Ray Villafane's PUMPKINS

Ray Villafane's PUMPKINS

Photographs by Ray Villafane

GIBBS SMITH
TO ENRICH AND INSPIRE HUMANKIND

First Edition
16 15 14 13 12   5 4 3 2 1

Text and photographs © 2012 Ray Villafane

Published by
Gibbs Smith
P.O. Box 667
Layton, Utah 84041

1.800.835.4993 orders
www.gibbs-smith.com

Designed by Renee Bond
Printed and bound in Hong Kong
Gibbs Smith books are printed on paper produced from
sustainable PEFC-certified forest/controlled wood source.
Learn more at www.pefc.org.

Library of Congress Control Number: 2012937606

ISBN 13: 978-1-4236-2426-4

This book is dedicated to my dearly departed mother,
Virginia Villafane, who had big dreams for me . . .
Here you go, Mommy.

ACKNOWLEDGMENTS

A tremendous thanks goes to all of my students in Bellaire Schools, for their excitement and encouragement that made the whole experience fun for me. Much thanks goes to Russell Bolt, of Bolt Farms in Ellsworth, Michigan, for providing me with many years of ideal pumpkins for my early carvings. A big thanks also goes to Gerald Johnson of Johnson Farms in Saginaw, Michigan, for the pumpkin opportunities through the years as well. More recent thanks goes to Darryl Pierce in New Zealand, for his hospitality in allowing me into his home as well as giving me free rein of his pumpkin patch. Huge gratitude goes to Wendy and the Aiello family for their gracious donations of the "picks of the litter" at the outstanding Uesugi Pumpkin Farm in San Martin, California, which incidentally provides the most perfect pumpkins for my carving style! And finally, my family, for the countless years of having to endure pumpkin guts and shavings stuck to the bottoms of their feet for several weeks out of each year. And, of course, Gibbs Smith, Publisher, for giving me the opportunity to share my best in print with the world.

INTRODUCTION

The evolution of a Ray Villafane pumpkin began in the mid-90s, when I was a kindergarten through twelfth grade teacher for thirteen years. Early in my teaching career, a student brought in a large pumpkin he had grown and asked me to carve it for him. The end result was fairly crude, but it was the beginning of something that would grow far beyond the classroom. From that point on, each fall the kids brought in pumpkins for me to carve. Many mornings I would be greeted with a dozen or more pumpkins sitting in front of my classroom door, each with a note asking if I could carve he or she, this or that. This went on for years.

I eventually resigned from teaching to become a full-time commercial sculptor, sculpting high-end collectibles and toys for companies such as DC Comics, Marvel, MacFarlane Toys, and Hasbro. It was at this point that my pumpkin carvings really took off. I began to approach the pumpkins with the same intensity and passion that I gave my professional sculpting work, despite knowing that they would likely rot away in a week. These creations quickly became some of my most cherished pieces of art. At the end of the day, they just seemed magical to me. For a brief moment in time, the pumpkins take on lives of their own. I often think that if the yellow brick road had led Dorothy to a pumpkin patch, she would encounter the very pumpkins I have become so addicted to carving. They are just plain old fun to look at, and it is my hope that you find the same magic and joy in these pumpkins that I do.

Over the years, the pumpkins have led to many great opportunities. Above all, I would have to say that catching the attention of my beautiful wife was probably the most noteworthy. I am so grateful for her encouragement to take my sculpting further, and, more importantly, for her good nature when it came to the pumpkin guts and shavings being tracked through the house every fall.

HOW TO CARVE A PUMPKIN

Here is an abbreviated tutorial on how to block in a simple pumpkin face using strictly loop tools.

The majority of my carvings are done without the use of any sharp tools, such as a knife. I typically use a knife only to tighten up details and creases at the end. Utilizing loop tools allows you to execute various contours that would otherwise be very difficult to achieve.

When carving a pumpkin in a 3-D manner, be sure to choose a pumpkin that is heavy for its size. This higher relative weight indicates that it is likely thicker than other pumpkins of similar size. The thickness will allow you to dig in deep without breaking through the rind, which is important because the deeper you push, the more the nose and other features seem to pop out!

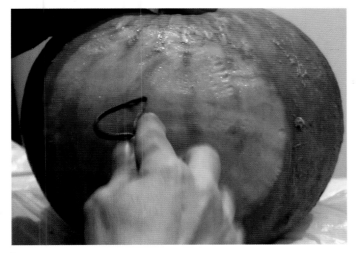

1. Using the wide, flat side of a large loop tool, scrape off the rind from the face of the pumpkin.

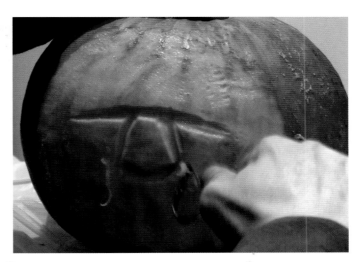

2. Using the pointed side of the loop tool, establish the brow line and parameters of the nose.

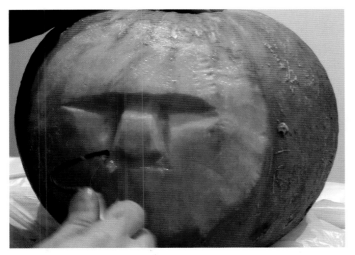

3. Remove material below the brow in order to define each eye socket. The bridge of the nose should also be taken down in order to create a "slope" that leads toward the tip of the nose. The area on the tip of the nose should be preserved and not carved away. This will ensure that the nose sticks out, thus creating a strong 3-D look. The eye-cavity sockets should gently taper to blend into the cheeks.

4. Using the point of your loop tool, create smile line creases that originate from the lower outer nasal area and extend out and down toward the lower portion of the pumpkin. Remove some of the pumpkin material in this area so that the area below the nose sits deeper, reinforcing a protruding nose. Also taper the pumpkin deeper as you approach the smile lines, essentially establishing a muzzle area that sits slightly recessed.

5. Scribe in a smile and soften some of the features. Be sure to give a slope to the nose.

6. Using the pointed side of a medium-sized loop, push the creases of the smile farther back. In the eye-socket areas, remove some material below the eyes to create "bags." Dig slightly deeper near the tear ducts as well as the outer eye areas. Doing so will help reinforce spherical-shaped eyes. You may also give the indication of wrinkles extending onto the bridge of the nose as well as "crow's feet" on the outer ends of the eyes. The crease for the actual meeting of the upper and lower eyelid can be scribed in with a very small pointed loop.

7. Continue to refine the contours and creases with the medium-sized loop.

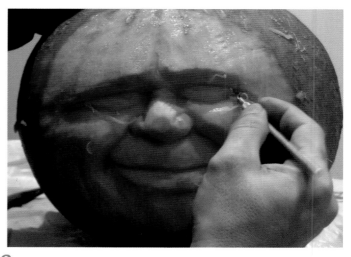

8. Using your small pointed loop, tighten up and sharpen the creases within the mouth as well as eyes.

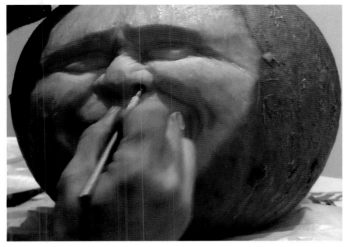

9. Using the small rounded loop, remove material at the base of the nose in order to define the nostrils.

10. Using the large loop, gently work the surface to smooth unwanted imperfections. A green dish-scouring pad works magic for this step as well.

All finished!

Trying to explain how to carve a pumpkin in ten easy steps is challenging. Hopefully, this little tutorial inspired you to give it a try and you'll have relative success. If you would like to follow a series of in-depth video tutorials, you can visit my website at www. villafanestudios.com for more information. The two-disc video tutorial contains four detailed tutorials geared toward multiple skill levels, from the artistically challenged to the professional sculptor.

Watch blank pumpkins come alive before your eyes!

THE PUMPKINS

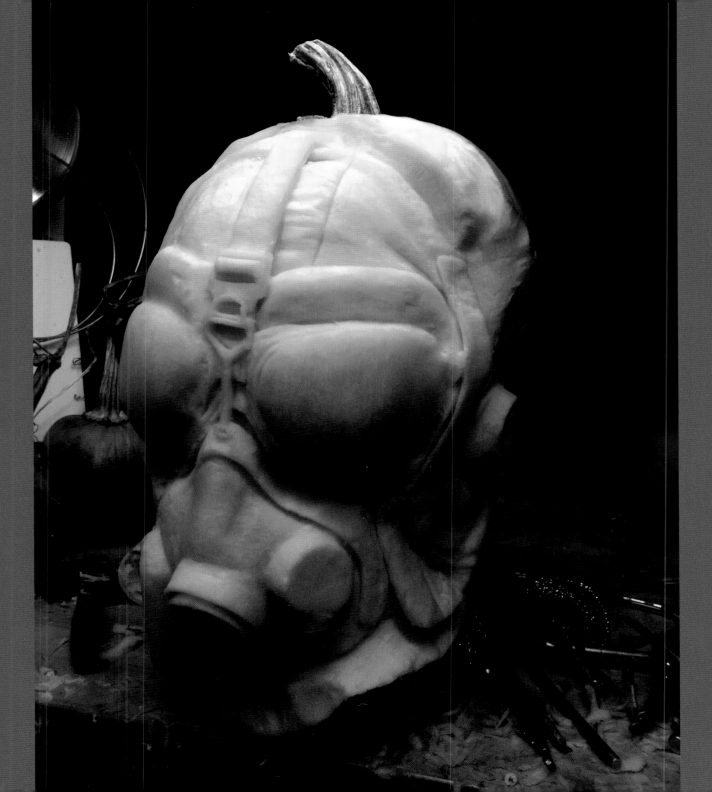

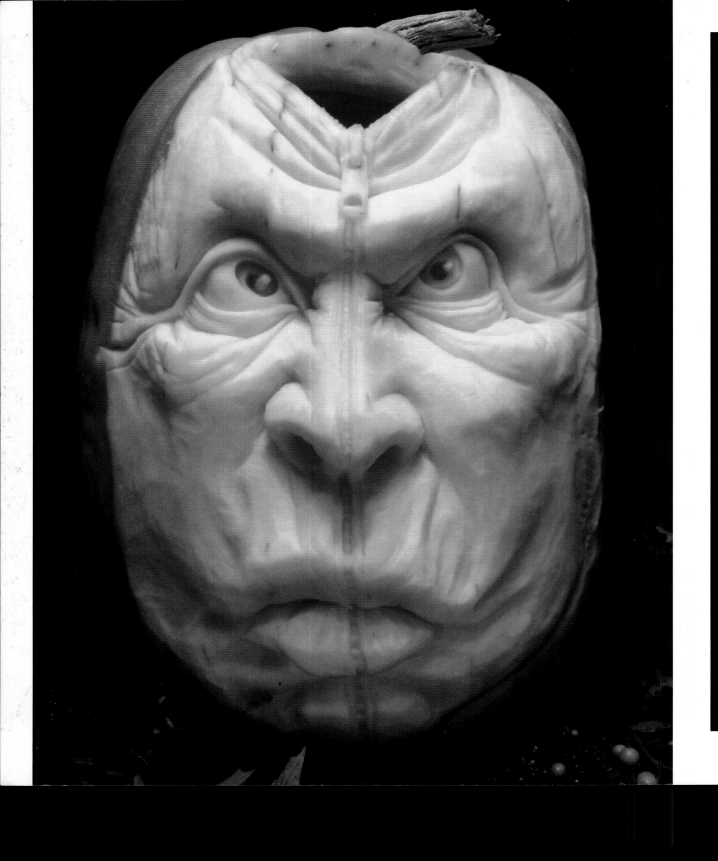

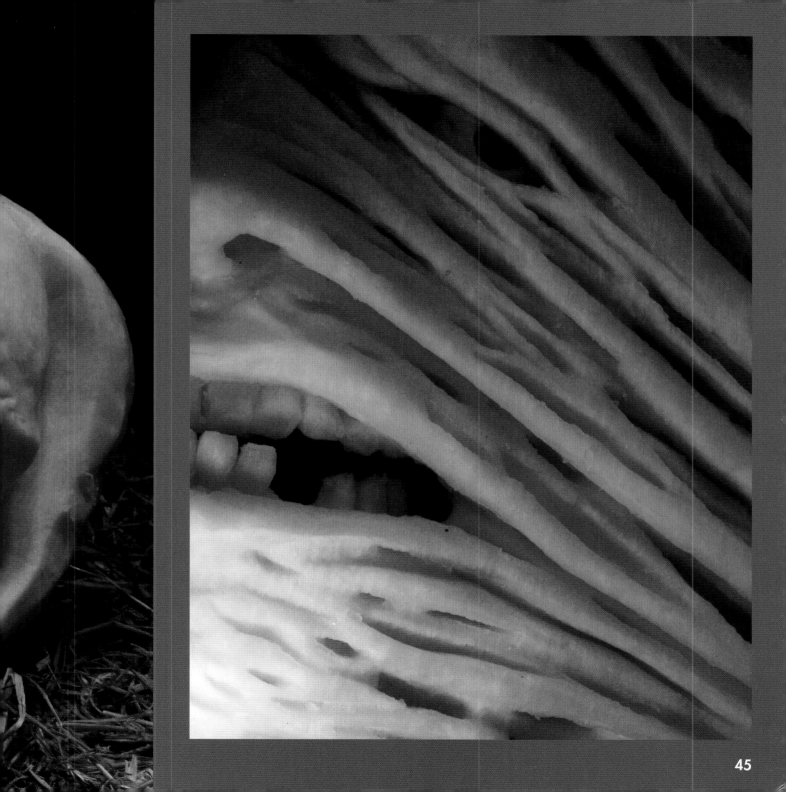

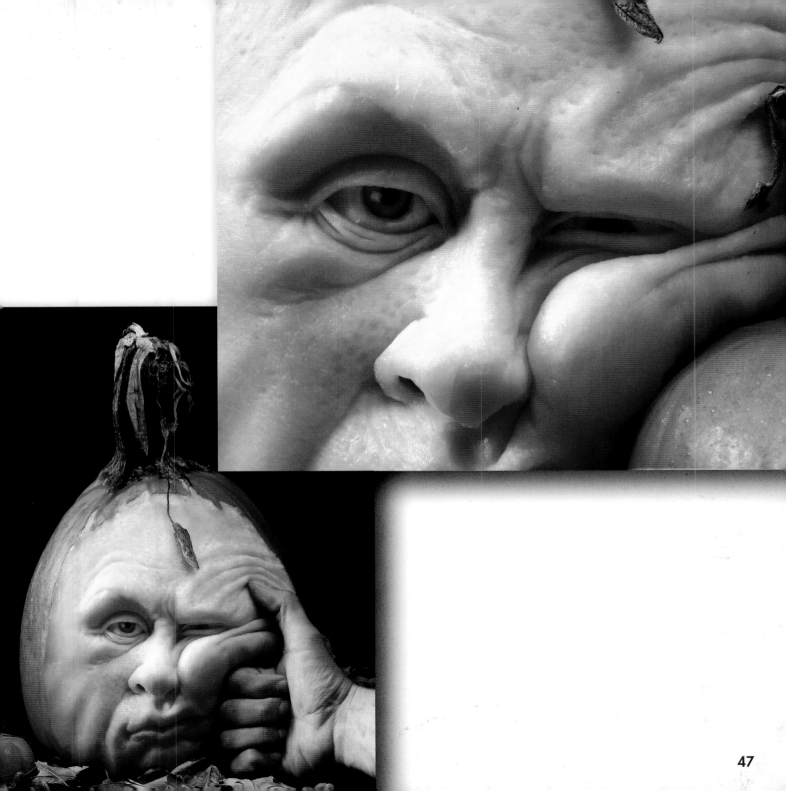

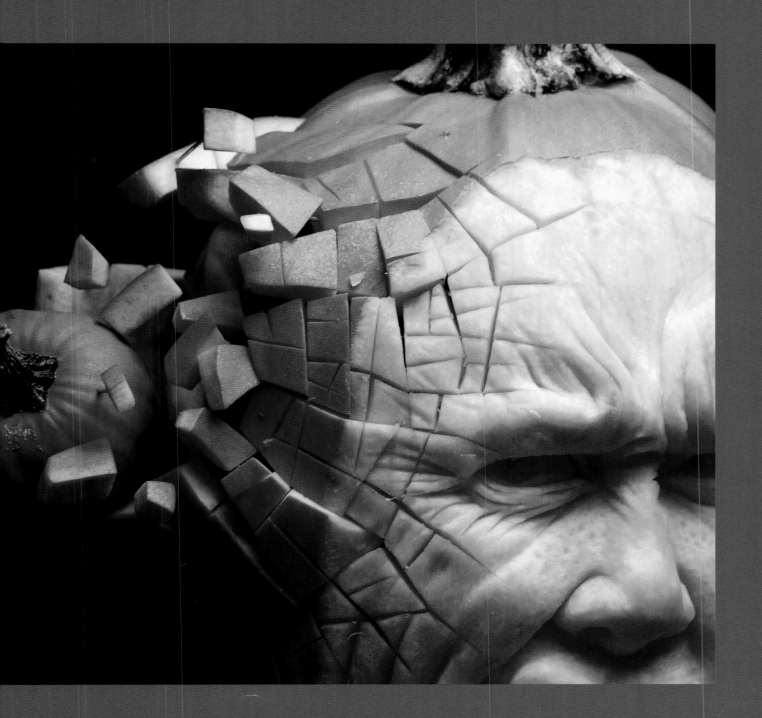

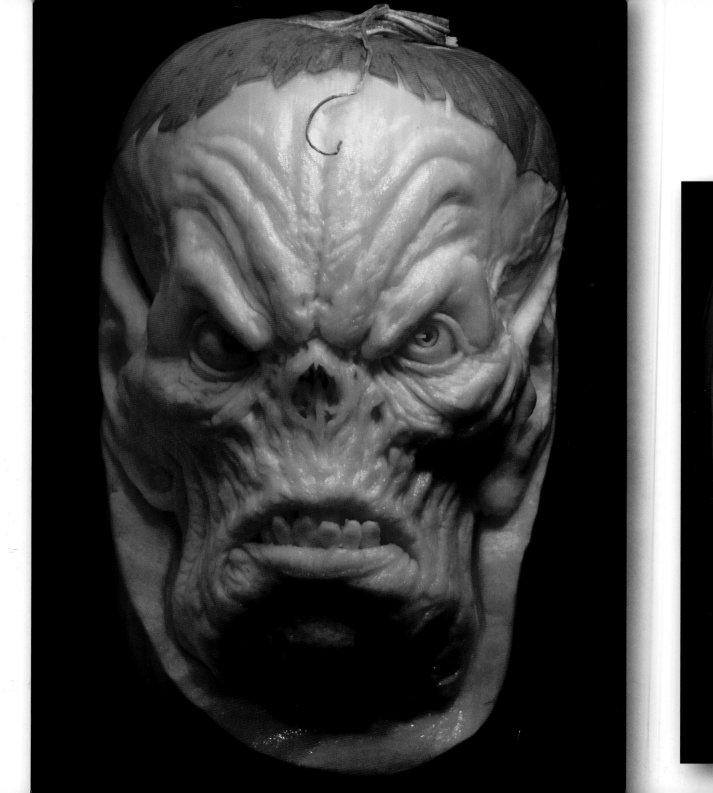

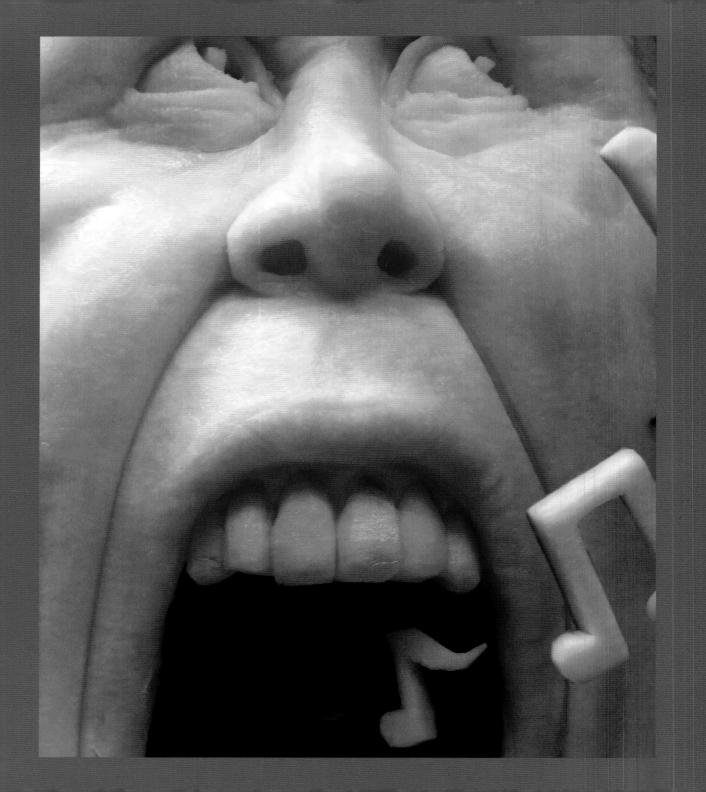

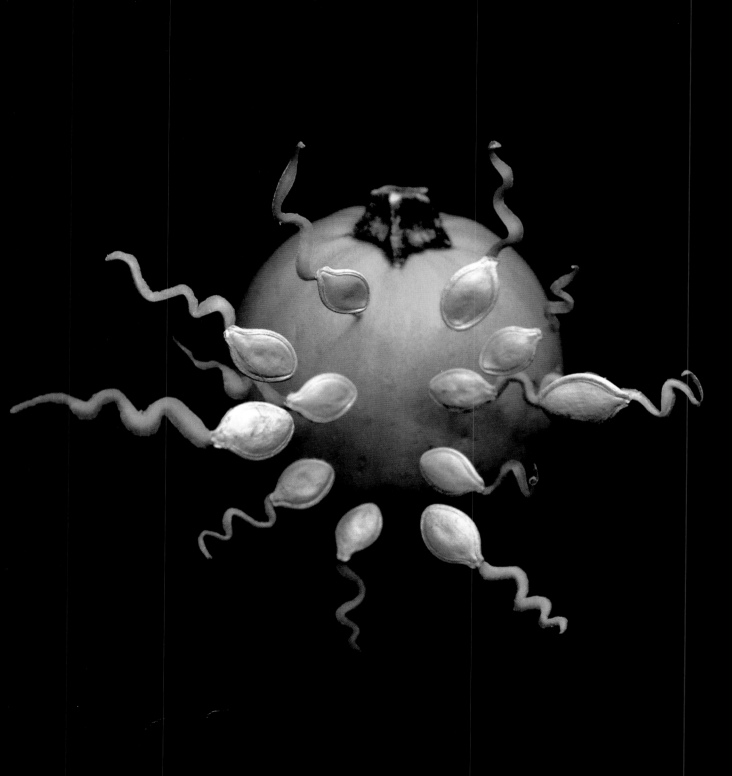

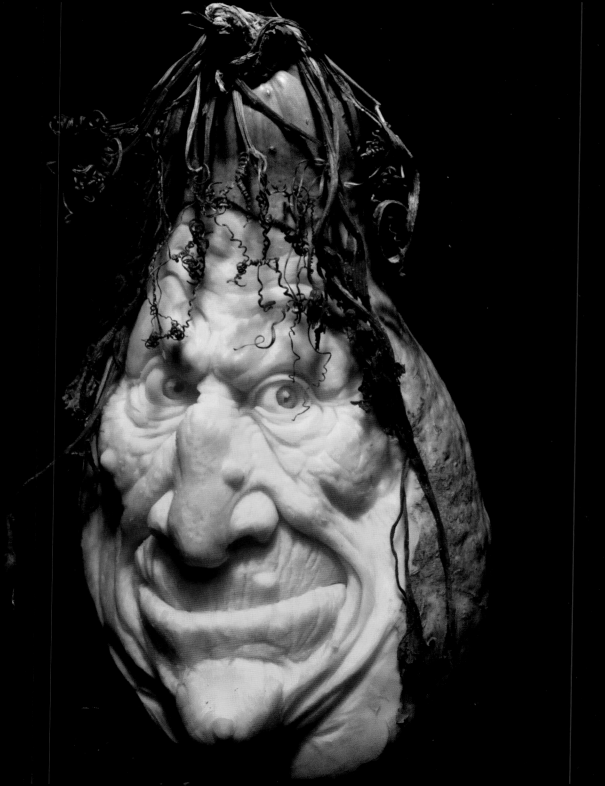

Villafane Studios

Ray Villafane's 3-D Pumpkin Carving Tutorials

Four complete pumpkin carving tutorials!
Tutorials for everyone from beginner to expert.
Pumpkin vine arm tutorial, photo gallery,
time-lapse videos of carvings and more!

2 DVD Set

Carved pumpkin replicas

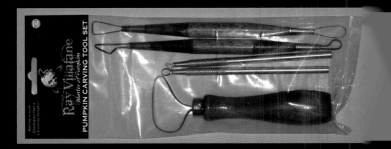

Visit www.villafanestudios.com for information on ordering
DVD tutorial, tool kit, prints, replicas, apparel and more.